DATE DUE

JAN 1 7 2006			
GAYLORD			PRINTED IN U.S.A.

Honey and Junk

DANA GOODYEAR

Honey and Junk

W. W. NORTON & COMPANY   *New York • London*

For information about permission to reproduce selections from this book,
write to Permissions, W. W. Norton & Company, Inc.,
500 Fifth Avenue, New York, NY 10110

Manufacturing by the Courier Companies, Inc.
Book design by Julia Druskin
Production manager: Andrew Marasia

Library of Congress Cataloging-in-Publication Data

Goodyear, Dana.
Honey and junk / Dana Goodyear.— 1st ed.
p. cm.
ISBN 0-393-06006-3 (hardcover)
I. Title.
PS3607.O5923H66 2005
811'.6—dc22

2004028375

W. W. Norton & Company, Inc.
500 Fifth Avenue, New York, N.Y. 10110
www.wwnorton.com

W. W. Norton & Company Ltd.
Castle House, 75/76 Wells Street, London W1T 3QT

1 2 3 4 5 6 7 8 9 0

For my parents
M.A.M. and L.R.G. (1936-2001)

Contents

I.

II.

The author wishes to thank the editors of the journals in which these poems originally appeared.

The New Yorker: "Awake and Dreaming," "On Love," "Sleeping Cure," "County Line Road," "Incarnation," "Old Saybrook," "Dream of Safety," "The Undressing Paradox," "Oasis," and "Day and Age"

New York Times Book Review: "Fluke"

The New York Review of Books: "Verboten" and "Sleep Talk"

The Yale Review: "Umbra" and "Raised by Aliens"

The Paris Review: "Flagrance"

Open City: "Things get better before they get worse," "Séance at Tennis," "Oracle," and "Setting"

The American Poetry Review: "Over Your Dead Body," "Safe House I–V," "Houseguests," "Double Jeopardy," and "My MO"

Slate: "Ruminant," "Envelope," and "Cape"

I.

Things get better before they get worse

I find you drinking bourbon
with a teenager—
let's not leave her out of this,
or the fact that you don't drink.

I command a river view,
and like a widow watch the boats;
my roommates trot their babies out
to make a wet nurse out of me.

Are you listening?
(No time for that—now let his hand
go at the fat part of your leg.
Now be a good girl and go back to bed.)

A stranger on the answering machine:
"I think I've got *exactly* what you're looking for.
Tons of light; water on three sides."
They ask after you at the garage;
I tell them little lies.

Séance at Tennis

I play with an old boyfriend, to tease you out.
In white shorts that you've never seen before.
You storm—wind, panic in the tree.
Rattling like the genius
like the jealous man.
Making it impossible to hit.
So nothing clears the net.
An inside joke, my comingback love:
He can't return, but you can?

After an hour, the court is swept, and reassumes
the waiting face of the bereft. But *you*—
the sky turns blue with your held breath.

Shield the Joyous

We took a white blanket to the grass,
out of view of the landscape
architect and his crew.
The air smelled hot and small
stings bore down on us.
Afterward, of course, we ate the fruit.
We couldn't help ourselves.

Verboten

The godless lick of the electric fence
to which you offered your left hand.
Your winded bloodred shirt,
oxygenated like the tissue of the poppies
I'm not supposed to talk about.
The one in which you were my brother;
in which you scavenged crabshells from the trash;
in which I met the dreamgirls
with their long blond hair
and saw they had inherited your scars.

The line cut out and cut again.
The train had left,
I heard its futile three-note human song.
It set you off, you were that live.

Bermuda

We were on vacation
so tried new sex.

The dark clot of your hair
and your pained, drunk eyes
have blotted out the rest.

We went down with equipment
and saw a school of bottles
six feet under, where water mothers them.

I can hear my father,
buzzing the shore in his plane.
He knows I'm here.

The little silver fish are licking us.
They are merest slipping edges
of what we have not grasped.

Over Your Dead Body

This wasn't what you had in mind
when you said, A house by the sea—
this flat Japanese plan; this expanse
that stubs on a bunker of grass;
these swans hissing humans off the nest;
and vitex, the abortion tree, scratching at the window screen.

I don't think my mother was part of your ideal.
Or this dinner of wet chicken lobster and gin.
You meant Sweden, a kind of sober heaven
where you wouldn't have to think about God.
Stay, stunt love, if you can stand it here.
Soon your double body will be nobody, no more.

Double Vision

I feel a shadow watching
when I comb my hair.
You are backlit in the reading chair.

I keep asking where and where.
There, there. No, there there.

Oracle

At the foot of your bed one night:
the murderer, a wolf, the grift,
the apparition with an open mouth
and flawless teeth.
The type that stops at nothing
to say its little bit.
After that: "I had a dream I had to tell you I was dead."
I used to think illogic kept me safe.
You sure told me.

When your heart stopped the black dog
choked on a finial from the baby's bassinet,
and the all-night crying started up in vain.

Oneiric

During the days of the dreams of the boarding-school wars,
in which I watched all my generation
slingshotted to death, while I read Rupert Brooke,

I remembered a winter party
with a Middle Eastern theme:
your cigarette burned a way
through the pink cocoon
costuming my head.

You weren't there for the dreams—they came later,
when the dirty tree was yellowing
and the honey crystalled in the jar,
and your sealed rooms, as I imagined them,
grew hotter every hour.

Awake and Dreaming

Don't cry. You're inside
the island chiropractor's dream.
Let the muscles go, the heart,
the pulsing brain,
the mesmerism of the animal terrain.
No knowing, where we're going.
Send me some intelligence.
Be the sleeper in the field.

Ruminant

I will trot you out
on your cold feet
to see the frost
in the field,
covered in childish flowers
when we last spoke.
I will coddle you like a cow
with her last meal,
and open everything up
that tries to heal.

On Love

I go back to the room and the room is the same.
Terrified lightbulbs burn through the day.
The blood caught in your outspread arm
hangs like frozen blooms, a dipped love bough.

On the roof above: heat and seed pool
in the dark upholstery and flowers burn up in their beds.
There were times I woke up laughing from my sleep.
The thick white smell of clethra makes me think of this.

You want your body back and so come thudding
into mine—gorge the veins
and pull the blood down to my gut—
toll the base of my neck—beat my cussed heart.

I am at the office! so please, no more coming
on to me. Sex makes me seasick—
the cold chopped sea and nauseous hungriness—
the axe in ice, the shaft that opened when you died.

Sleeping Cure

Where will you go if—?
The major arteries
and avenues are closed.
We are too cumbersome
to tunnel out—yes, fat
—besides, there's been an accident.
And—why am I always the last to know?
You're dead.

Sleep, little lamb.
Give up the honey and junk,
at least for the duration.
I will tell the story
of your afterlife.
It takes place in a lit tent
in a blackening room.
It begins with a consummation scene.

II.

Raised by Aliens

I come to in an avocado tub: Cuyahoga, Vitabath,
six o'clock, a Saturday, the comet year.
Through the sliding glass I see a field of igloos
and a straining dog who can't come in,
because his rope-red tail thrashes the majolica
from every high-shine demilune.
Mother's vacuuming, a black hole, knowing
nothing happens here. Her eyeshadow a gibbous moon.
In an Astro I become a flickering defibrillator storm.
Father in his glowing mask. He was forty, I was born.

County Line Road

Who was Father—a bandage, a mustache,
from time to time a saddening salt-and-pepper beard.
Mother? Some sort of monger—I see her with a pink fish,
my bodyweight, dill hairs clinging to her hands.
"Daddy is tired," I am said to have said,
and then I'd sing to him, sleeping.
He was an athlete, dislocated. He said, Forget Me Not.
Mother was never in the same room with any of us.
I think she was a hostess, in which case I should say,
Thank you for having me.

The Lion in the Igloo

The winter it snowed fifteen feet,
our dog, like a circus bear,
broke the chain and crashed
the cover of a neighbor's pool.
Of the log cabin I can say:
foxes found the rabbits caged in there.
Soon we went our separate ways.
At the pueblo of Acoma,
the oldest inhabited village in the United States,
I climbed into a ceremonial pit:
just as I had hidden in the closet
when she came home from ikebana class,
or sleepwalked to their bed
when they had gone to France,
waking to a policeman's
flashlight in my eye.
Of my parents: being in the orchard
without them was like not being in the orchard at all.
When it came to their belongings,
everything good was made of Midas gold.
The long process of becoming them began.
His next wedding night: a light inside a paper bag.
The teenagers ate acid; I tried to be the perfect flower girl.
The adobe burner, with its tiny painted ladder
and a dark smudge at the core
is that whole world.

Second-Marriage Pork

1. PETRA

The girl has everything: German measles,
slender limbs, access to pornography,
a box of gold-butt cigarettes, a flat.
A mother wearing diamonds
in the kitchen after dark,
saying *Schatzieputzie*
while she heats the bedtime milk.

2. THE MEWS HOUSE

My mother's making Second-Marriage Pork,
food of newlyweds;
the "I've gone to live with Petra" note
has gone unread.
A birthright yellow nightie in the window
of the temporary third-floor room
is risen like a honeymoon.

Incarnation

In the blind a bird dog watches
as you become irretrievable
and snow geese come down from the east.
Your children look for you where you are not.
In the basement of the house.
The ties we find are drunk with animal life:
the pheasants set in whiskey-colored frieze.
Heavy English jackets laid like skins.
My milk teeth in a drawer.

I taste you in smoked meat near the bone.
My lungs run, sick and guttural and gold.
You faced an animal. He said, "It hurts so much."

Derelict

Sudden as the living dove beneath
the brake pedal
that scared you half to death—
somehow I didn't feel you go.
A blanket fear for the one who
was lying next to me.
It was him or you, then both.

Message

How long can this last.
I've heard they build the obsolescence in.
Is this more like a tripwire
or a fuse.
If I handle it right
may I keep you?

I call again for your old-sounding voice,
recorded when you were here last fall
and bleeding uncontrollably.

You pick up.
And again, when I am in your house,
and don't answer the phone.
It has always been true
that anyone who wants to talk to me
must go through you.

Pine

This is your pine
overcoat, as they say,
and its gray bark buckles
like a loosened skin.
The skeleton
shrugs and points all ways.
When?
You never know.
The elk descend,
the stars pull back into their holes.
In morning, you seep through the snow.

Setting

The islands, locals say, drift
from year to year. In the overwhelming wake,
their matte-gold grasses disappear
like bracelets begged from dreams
slip from the dreamer's wrist.

Frequently I have said
in my not-quite-human voice,
flooded, as it were, with relief:
Thank God I had a chance to tell you
before it was too late.
Once you said, to put an end to it:
No. *I* told *you*.
Don't you find some conversations
make it difficult to sleep.

We find ourselves, again,
in the wet and flavored woods.
Hear everywhere untrustable cries.
The angles of cranes
pulling dark strings across the sky.
The governance of shadows—
this year, every year, the same and not the same.
The shapeshift of the absence
that goes by our name.

Birthday

I would call you specially
to tell you about Peru
and the wax-jacket men I saw there
who remind even themselves of you.

And how I felt diminished
in a Midtown shop for gentlemen's clothes
with so many imitations
in so many not-you rows.

If it all seemed endless
viewed in the three-way mirror
then I remember the opposite endlessness
when you were still much clearer.

Beechcraft

We trembled like ice
in a milk punch sky.
This was years before
this father died.
I squinted at the Chesapeake
and at the green-black hidey-holes
of the houses on the bay.
I smelled the grass,
the gasoline, the greenhoused instruments.
After this I only looked
for what would swallow me alive.

Three Takes

I touched my father's pink, untroubled cheek
and neither of us flinched.

He picked up something from a loose dirt bed:
the rust of childhood.

A mother bird was sick in the nest;
Jake gently fished her out.

Like a mouth, I grew right over;
quiet as a can of worms,
I took in everything.

Envelope

I got one from the widow,
no note, just a key.
I sent one to the widower
and it arrived empty.
He got one from a friend
already dead in '43,
then came home to deliver
six thousand boom babies.

I came to you too late,
too little, too ungenerously.
Your heart was bloody full
when I begged it to take care of me.

The Causeway

Katharine Hepburn has never waved hello.
And yet you're at the window,
with your cigarette, red,
and coral in the leg,
and your offering of marmalade
made from fourteen-carat gold.
A varicose of garnet in the gray beach stone.
Your breath in December drifting toward the Sound.

Old Saybrook

Pour the bourbon
in a scallop shell
and leave it on the porch,
but know that she's flown south.

Gone, but not to Florida.
As I sleep she reaches
for me with elderly, cured hands.

Her sandals curl by the back door,
white leather peeling from the sole
like afterdeath fingernails unfolding
in the last mute wave of growing old.

Dream of Safety

Expiration comes no matter what we do.
No mindfulness forestalls the serial
slough and clockwork days of burial.
It's end-rhymed slogans that ring doubly true.

We are not safe in numbers, not safe two by two.
What it is hard to know, we misconstrue.
And human love and unison are null
when even solitude is terminal.

Abandon, please, the fiction of the will,
for gone is gone for good or ill.
Our dead stream by and streak the water blue.
Don't let the smell of burning comfort you.

Safe House I

Call it what you will.
It isn't what it used to be—
or, what it never was—
once they kick the door
and sit you down
for the what-did-you-know-and-when.
This is an arrest?
All eyes jerk toward the evidence.
Some life, one whispers,
fingering the spools
of blood and treasure
spilled out on the bedroom floor.

Safe House II

Constancy, anguish.
Under the old blue dome.
A garden for the fleeing
marks the dead end of the road.

Now that no one's listening
lead your secrets from their stall.
No need to answer quickly.
No urgency at all.

Safe House III

It's worth a detour
to the Villa of the Mysteries.
Here they found a man
near the basement door
with a key in his hand.
His slave held all the jewelry.
In all, there are two thousand bodies at the site.
"But where did they bury the survivors?"
The other eighteen thousand, would you believe it,
still live today, in unimaginable happiness,
just down the road.
It doesn't take a genius to say,
Get out while you can.
It takes an optimist.

Safe House IV

In the courtyard was a fountain
where you damaged
your first watch,
bluing it, brainwashing it,
holding it under until it stopped.
There went all the time in the world.
Who wouldn't scream for that.

Soon she left you,
and, later, left you the house.

Safe House V

Trust me, this place is going to make your life.
The animals don't bite,
they just contribute to the karmic atmosphere.
I know what you are thinking:
the answer's an emphatic *No*.
Even if we wanted to.

You may remember So-and-so—
"mysteriously disappeared while on a fishing trip"?
Last seen snowboarding in France.
The grandmother known as No. 5
is forty-two again and just divorced.
Your old man's in the wind.

III.

Fluke

Don't go—let me explain.
There's no one else.
Just this hanger-on,
eating in the dark and fearing
for its life. For the life of me
I can't get rid of it.
It's feeding at the heartmeat,
making scrimshaw of the bone.

Pupil

In a dumbshow of affection
I moved the candle slightly to the side,
and said a silent thanks-be-god
for leaning in confidingly
and all the other oldest tricks.
Then lightly tapping on the glass
to signal for more wine
I told you all you'd need to know.
What you see in there is only a reflection.
In the sinkhole at the center of the eye
is a disappearance bag,
a dark hood for the hanging,
portable, and light in its own way.

The Undressing Paradox

My phantom companion
speaks German
and tells me to strip.

In one encounter he had ice-blue feet
and a fixed expression on his face.
The interpretation: I am letting go.

The drift is this.
Give the hypothermic girl
a stiff hot drink.
The mouth of a stranger is a pocket of breathable air.
The spit is a warm vital flow.

Cape

Take me to your sleeping porch!
Cross-breeze. Swiss dot. View.
We'll try for some rude
healthful pure,
do what young people do.

Or, I'll point out scenery,
the more expensive property.
A slurry beach.
An empty breach.
Thick, eggish water breaking
on the boring, boring shore.

Is everything defective here?
There are men downstairs who think
that gin's a breakfast drink.

I mean to say: It's May.
Let's find an outdoor shower.

Houseguests

From time to time the propers come.
They sleep in every bed,
eat bacon & butter on very thin white bread.
Play bocce on the golf course,
fuck like goats
while the bodies in the river drink their boats.

Shuck, girls, shuck!
(The heart ducks out and stuffs the sheets.)
The rain is coming down tonight.
They're coming back.
Quick: lips to the mirror,
family jewels to the drain.
Just stay still—you won't remember anything.

Flagrance

Where in heaven have you been?
Wreathed waif, pale grace,
Scandalous would-be.

You've painted your room gold, I see.
It's in your hair.
I hate to mention it.

Wasn't there something . . . about a check?
The doorknobs rattle restlessly—
Spring wind.

Your blazer helps explain.
The more things change . . .
You excuse yourself, needing liquid personality.

Here and everywhere:
The godforsaken smell
Of last-legs hyacinth—dirt sweet.

Umbra

We share a habit of accepting hospitality.
Count a blessing, mix a drink—instant indispensability.
You are (you stir) *relaxed*, on novel number three.

English major, accent minor.
Trace. Ohio crossed with stroke of luck—
to other manners born.

It smells like heaven here.
Clover mown, clever man.
O kept bohemian—come walk with me.

See, on the potato fields, a haze.
They're up for sale by Sotheby's.
Estates already named: Duplex Oblige, Feigned Ease.

At night, the floodlights silver
These new-minted trees.
White ash. Prefabricated legacies.
Not bad for weekend company.

The right place at the right time

Last night, a hot wind tore the glass
from a table on the balcony
of your month-to-month hotel.
You were lying, I am sure,
on the yellow bedspread,
with furious insomnia.
You ordered ham and brie.

I was in a neo-Gothic church
with cold gray sugar walls
owlishly examining
the who the why the why.
While picturing the bulkhead
of the river trees fleshed out in green,
it came to me. I should let you be.

Sleep Talk

You say there's no hypocrisy in sleep,
and that is when they turned on us.
Went into the closet
and dragged us like some puppets
through the street.
Like animals with human
newborns in their mouths.
Was I supposed to hold the leash?

And I woke up, the pose of love—
My God like I had left you on the stove.

"Touch the Walls of Your House for Luck"

When leaving: tap, tap, tap,
on the marble slabs whose patterns
look like butcher stains.
Never see it again.
Tap the baby learning to talk
who bathes in the sink
three floors beneath the junkie
in his oatmeal tub. What she doesn't know.
Kiss your sweetheart; draw that liquor in.
Say a quick, forgettable goodbye.
Don't call out to the shape on the dark street
unless you know when it will answer back.

Double Jeopardy

You have no roof.
Someone calls you from the shelterdeck
to deliver the bad news.
There's an unofficial custom in this country
you have travelled to, they tell you, way too late,
and now the captain's heading for the Gulf of Finland
and the worst storm he can find.
What ever happened to cover of night?
Remember, it's the summer equinox,
you who wanted it this way.
Everybody has to live.
And so with little fanfare,
and in the upwardly expanding white,
you slip from reach.

Miracles happen.
After that, your plane goes down
in a popular vacation spot.
Your life line stops you short.
Your heart gives out.
Hand to mouth is how I take this in.

My MO

You imagined all your walls
outfitted in leopard skin.
This is what I call hiding in plain view.
Simultaneously, I was imagining
a make-out session in the basement
of the house in Maryland;
my yellow skirt and underwear
trailed straight to our nest.
Sorry, our *love* nest.
Not long after that I found a man
of the approximate shape and age
in a sold-out lecture hall.
I saw inside his mouth;
he wasn't the person I was looking for.

Pan, as you know,
is a radio signal for distress.
Deadpan, then, is what you get
when you have no other choice.

Modern

There is no squalid here,
no after me comes the flood.
(No flood.) Fruits aren't dying on the vine;
the plants are babyless and silk.
Like an afterlife: you, the walls, in white,
"drenched" in light. Me, the prehistoric:
hoarding, bleeding, blackening the pan
like the long-haired wife you never wanted
and now can't even stand.

Oasis

We found (like the deserting) spacious calm,
drank a pair of Arnold Palmers underneath a palm.
Went for massage and mud, lacquer, love,
overheated minerals, a stimulating rub.
Then—as if it could be used, as if for art—
I placed a grain of doubt in your open-pored heart,
and watched what had been small dilate
and everything else evaporate.

Hurricane

In the underground city, "Oh Danny Boy"
was played on a saw.
Upstairs the traffic lights rocked on their necks;
glass doors were pinned against the walls.
The violence spoke. It said, Welcome to My World.
Children, pushed, were little offerings,
the bones wrapped in the fat. The trees were elderly;
their wigs blew off, they threw their hands into the air.
People screamed into their phones
and gave themselves away. *I love you!*
I can't hear you. I'll call you back, OK?
In the subway there was dancing, signs of hope.
Real-live men were marrying good-looking dolls,
a crowd had gathered, money was exchanged.
Someone, celebrating, beat a plastic drum.

Day and Age

Skimming by,
the milky spill of my old eye,
the mute white cat
now skirts me at the store.
Retarded and alert.

What good are instincts anymore?
Who does the math
for lengths of desperation
and how far to the door?

A woman, pregnant
like a red wool bud,
is circling the rink.
Catastrophe, I think.

Notes

"Second-Marriage Pork": *Schatzieputzie* is a German endearment.

"Beechcraft": Beechcraft is a make of airplane.

"Dream of Safety": The title is from W. H. Auden's "Leap Before You Look."

"Safe House III": The Villa of the Mysteries is at Pompeii.

"The Undressing Paradox": The title refers to the tendency of a freezing person to think he's very hot and take off all his clothes. This and other symptoms of hypothermia referred to are from Peter Stark's *Last Breath: Cautionary Tales from the Limits of Human Endurance.*

"Touch the Walls of Your House for Luck": The title is from Stephen Vincent Benét's "John Brown's Body."